United States Government Accountability Office

GAO

Report to the Ranking Member,
Committee on Homeland Security,
House of Representatives

March 2012

FEDERAL PROTECTIVE SERVICE

Better Data on Facility Jurisdictions Needed to Enhance Collaboration with State and Local Law Enforcement

GAO

Accountability ★ Integrity ★ Reliability

GAO-12-434

FEDERAL PROTECTIVE SERVICE

Better Data on Facility Jurisdictions Needed to Enhance Collaboration with State and Local Law Enforcement

Highlights of GAO-12-434, a report to the Ranking Member, Committee on Homeland Security, House of Representatives.

Why GAO Did This Study

The Department of Homeland Security's (DHS) Federal Protective Service (FPS) protects over 9,000 federal facilities under the custody and control of the General Services Administration (GSA). In 2007, FPS adopted an inspector-based workforce approach and indicated it would increase its reliance on state and local law enforcement agencies to respond to incidents at these facilities. These facilities range from facilities of proprietary or concurrent jurisdiction— where authority is shared by federal and state and local police—to facilities of exclusive jurisdiction, where only federal law enforcement has authority. As requested, this report assesses FPS's efforts to collaborate with state and local law enforcement for assistance in responding to incidents at these federal facilities. GAO reviewed documents on collaboration, GSA and FPS facility data, and GAO's work on key collaboration practices and internal control standards. GAO also contacted 73 selected state and local law enforcement agencies from geographic jurisdictions of varying population sizes and FPS buildings throughout the United States and interviewed FPS and GSA officials.

What GAO Recommends

In conjunction with the revised MOU that is being developed between GSA and FPS, GAO recommends the administrator of GSA ensure that efforts to identify the jurisdictions of all GSA buildings are completed and that these data are provided to FPS. GSA concurred with the recommendation.

View GAO-12-434. For more information, contact Mark L. Goldstein at (202) 512-2834 or goldsteinm@gao.gov.

What GAO Found

To collaborate with state and local law enforcement, the Federal Protective Service (FPS) uses memorandums of understanding (MOU), long-standing working relationships, written guidance to FPS staff, joint operations, and other initiatives. For example, FPS has MOUs ranging from sharing radio frequency usage in Alabama, to a mutual aid agreement with the Metropolitan Atlanta Rapid Transit Authority in Georgia. In some jurisdictions, such as the suburbs of the District of Columbia, FPS has no MOUs but has regular contact and long-standing mutual aid relationships with state and local law enforcement. To collaborate with state and local law enforcement, FPS has guidance that addresses issues such as the scope of law enforcement authorities on federal property and information sharing among jurisdictions. FPS established regional staff positions intended to improve collaboration with other organizations and has engaged in joint operations with state and local law enforcement. By comparison, other federal organizations with law enforcement responsibilities similar to FPS also use a variety of methods, ranging from the Department of Veterans Affairs' policy to seek MOUs with state and local law enforcement to the Smithsonian Institution's established relationships with the Metropolitan D.C. Police and others.

GAO found that state and local law enforcement organizations it contacted are generally willing to assist with incidents at federal facilities. For example, 48 of 52 respondents from state and local law enforcement agencies GAO contacted about this issue said that they would respond to a call at a federally owned facility; 27 said they had done so since 2007. Overall, the variety of efforts FPS has under way is consistent with the key collaboration practices GAO has previously identified and reflects a reasonable approach to collaboration, especially when combined with the willingness of state and local law enforcement to assist.

Although FPS has a reasonable approach to state and local collaboration, GAO found issues related to the quality of data exchanged between GSA and FPS on buildings and their locations. Through working groups, GSA is working with FPS to address these data inconsistency issues and is establishing a permanent GSA liaison at FPS's headquarters to improve data coordination. But as of the end of GAO's review, FPS still lacked complete data from GSA on the jurisdiction of about one third of the buildings it protects. GSA officials informed GAO that they are making progress with identifying building jurisdictions but were not yet in a position to provide complete information to FPS. These data are important because state and local law enforcement generally has no authority to enforce state and local law on properties of exclusive federal jurisdiction. An additional effect of not having these data is that FPS lacks assurance that in relying on state and local law enforcement to respond to incidents at federal facilities, it is not creating a situation where these entities may be exercising police authority where they lack such authority. As a result, incomplete jurisdictional data leaves FPS and state and local law enforcement less equipped to define and agree to respective roles and responsibilities when there are incidents at federal facilities.

Contents

Abbreviations

ADFO	Assistant Director for Field Operations
DHS	Department of Homeland Security
FPS	Federal Protective Service
GSA	General Services Administration
MOU	memorandums of understanding
MPD	Metropolitan Police Department
NPS	National Park Service
SI	Smithsonian Institution
VA	Department of Veterans Affairs
VAMC	Department of Veterans Affairs Medical Centers

United States Government Accountability Office
Washington, DC 20548

March 27, 2012

The Honorable Bennie G. Thompson
Ranking Member
Committee on Homeland Security
U.S. House of Representatives

Dear Mr. Thompson:

The Department of Homeland Security's (DHS) Federal Protective Service (FPS) protects over 9,000 federal facilities under the custody and control of the General Services Administration (GSA) by delivering integrated law enforcement and security services. To secure these buildings and safeguard their occupants, FPS employs about 1,225 federal staff, including law enforcement officers, investigators, and administrative personnel, and is responsible for management and oversight of approximately 14,000 contract security guards. These federal facilities range from facilities of proprietary or concurrent jurisdiction—in which authority is shared by federal and state and local police—to facilities of exclusive jurisdiction in which only federal law enforcement has authority. FPS conducts its mission by providing security services through two types of activities: (1) physical security activities, such as conducting risk assessments of GSA facilities and recommending risk-based countermeasures to GSA and tenant agencies aimed at reducing the likelihood and severity of incidents at facilities, and (2) law enforcement activities, such as responding to incidents, conducting criminal investigations, and exercising arrest authority. In order for FPS to track the continuous changes in the inventory of buildings that it protects—including new construction, disposed buildings, and over 8,000 leases—GSA, through its Public Buildings Service,[1] provides building data to FPS weekly from GSA's building property system.

---

[1]The Public Buildings Service acquires space on behalf of the federal government through new construction and leasing and acts as a caretaker for federal properties across the country.

In 2007, FPS adopted an inspector-based workforce approach to protect GSA-controlled facilities.[2] In testimony to Congress that same year, a DHS senior official stated that the agency was increasing its reliance on state and local law enforcement agencies to assist in responding to law enforcement incidents at these facilities as a way of ensuring that GSA buildings are adequately protected.[3] While FPS is statutorily responsible for enforcing federal laws and regulations for the protection of federal property and persons located on federal property regardless of the location, state and local law enforcement agencies are responsible for enforcing state laws and local ordinances within the particular state on concurrent and proprietary jurisdiction locations. In 2008, we recommended that FPS clarify roles and responsibilities of local law enforcement agencies in responding to incidents at GSA-controlled facilities.[4] Since this report was issued, FPS has issued specific agency instructions regarding coordination, hired new personnel to oversee coordination in the regions, and pursued additional memorandums of understanding (MOU)[5] when needed, such as in the case of clarifying roles and responsibilities between FPS and state and local law enforcement.

You asked us to provide an update on these issues. This report assesses FPS's efforts to collaborate with state and local law enforcement for assistance in responding to incidents at federal facilities. To meet this objective, we reviewed relevant documentation on federal facility building

---

[2]This model was intended to make more efficient use of FPS's declining staffing levels by increasing focus on FPS's physical security duties and consolidating law enforcement activities. FPS's goal was to shift its law enforcement workforce composition from a mix of about 40 percent police officers, about 50 percent inspectors, and about 10 percent special agents, to a workforce primarily composed of inspectors and some special agents. FPS's inspectors are responsible for law enforcement and security duties, including: patrolling building perimeters, responding to incidents, completing risk assessments for buildings, recommending security countermeasures, and overseeing the contract security workforce.

[3]Hearing on "Proposals to Downsize the Federal Protective Service and Effects on the Protection of Federal Buildings," Committee on Transportation and Infrastructure, U. S. House of Representatives, April 18, 2007.

[4]GAO, Homeland Security: The Federal Protective Service Faces Several Challenges That Hamper Its Ability to Protect Federal Facilities, GAO-08-683 (Washington, D.C.: June 11, 2008).

[5]For consistency, we are using the term MOU throughout this report for both memorandums of understanding (MOUs) and memorandums of agreement (MOAs).

data from GSA. In addition, we emailed a self-administered set of 22 structured questions to the heads of 73 state and local law enforcement agencies in jurisdictions throughout the United States that we determined had FPS-protected buildings. Our non-random selection of locations included varying population sizes served by the state and local law enforcement agencies located in a mixture of urban and rural areas as defined by the United States Department of Agriculture. We used the most recent Rural-Urban Continuum Codes.[6] We followed up our emails with phone calls to these state and local law enforcement agencies to obtain clarification of the responses as needed. Not every respondent answered every question. Although the results of our structured questionnaires cannot be generalized to the universe of jurisdictions that interact with FPS, the results provide key insights and illustrate how these organizations can help FPS respond to incidents.

Further, we interviewed GSA officials at GSA Headquarters in Washington, D.C. We also interviewed FPS officials at the Suitland, Maryland, and Battle Creek, Michigan, FPS MegaCenters[7] and toured the Suitland MegaCenter. We interviewed each of the 11 FPS Regional Directors to determine how their respective regions coordinate with state and local law enforcement agencies for the properties in their jurisdiction. For comparison with FPS, we contacted three federal agencies that provide their own law enforcement services at their facilities—the Department of Veterans Affairs, the Department of the Interior's National Park Service, and the Smithsonian Institution. We obtained relevant documents pertaining to their collaboration with state and local law enforcement and interviewed key officials. Lastly, we reviewed prior GAO work, including reports on key practices in interagency collaboration, facility protection, and internal controls. We also reviewed FPS data on buildings protected, staffing, procedures, and MOUs that are in place and

---

[6]Rural-Urban Continuum Codes form a classification scheme that distinguishes metropolitan (metro) counties by the population size of their metro area, and nonmetropolitan (nonmetro) counties by degree of urbanization and adjacency to a metro area or areas. See USDA Economic Research Service at http://www.ers.usda.gov/Briefing/Rurality/RuralUrbCon/.

[7]In 2000, the Federal Protective Service (FPS) transitioned all alarm-monitoring and dispatching capabilities from several regional control centers to four MegaCenters. Currently, each MegaCenter monitors multiple types of alarm systems, closed circuit television, and wireless dispatch communications within federal facilities throughout the nation. These centers—located in Michigan, Colorado, Pennsylvania, and Maryland—are equipped with state-of-the-art communication systems and operate continuously.

assessed the quality and completeness of these data. Collectively, this multifaceted approach enabled us to make conclusions about whether FPS's collaboration approach is reasonable. Appendix I contains more information on our objective, scope, and methodology.

We conducted this performance audit from February 2011 to March 2012 in accordance with generally accepted government auditing standards. Those standards require that we plan and perform the audit to obtain sufficient, appropriate evidence to provide a reasonable basis for our findings and conclusions based on our audit objectives. We believe that the evidence obtained provides a reasonable basis for our findings and conclusions based on our audit objectives.

Background

FPS—located within the National Protection and Programs Directorate[8] of DHS—protects the over 9,000 federal facilities that are under the control and custody of GSA, as well as the persons on those properties. FPS headquarters is located in Washington, D.C.; regional offices are located in New York, Boston, Philadelphia, Atlanta, Denver, Chicago, San Francisco, Seattle, Fort Worth, Kansas City, and the District of Columbia. FPS is authorized to enforce federal laws and regulations aimed at protecting GSA buildings and persons on the property and to investigate offenses against these buildings and persons.[9] These federal facilities include buildings of exclusive, concurrent, and proprietary jurisdictions.

- Exclusive: Under exclusive federal jurisdiction, the federal government—and federal law enforcement entities—have all of the legislative authority within the land area in question, while the state—and its state and local law enforcement entities—have no residual police powers.

---

[8]GAO, *Federal Protective Service: Progress Made but Improved Schedule and Cost Estimate Needed to Complete Transition,* GAO-11-554 (Washington, D C.: July 15, 2011).

[9]Section 1315(a) of Title 40, United States Code, provides that: "To the extent provided for by transfers made pursuant to the Homeland Security Act of 2002, the Secretary of Homeland Security...shall protect the buildings, grounds, and property that are owned, occupied, or secured by the Federal Government (including any agency, instrumentality, or wholly owned or mixed-ownership corporation thereof) and the persons on the property."

- Concurrent: In concurrent jurisdiction facilities, both federal and state governments—and law enforcement entities—have jurisdiction over the property.

- Proprietary: Under proprietary jurisdiction, the federal government has rights—similar to a private landowner—but also maintains its authorities and responsibilities as the federal government. Under proprietary jurisdiction, the local government is the principal municipal police authority.

To enable FPS to track changes in the inventory of federal buildings that it protects, GSA, through its Public Buildings Service, provides building data in electronic files to FPS weekly from GSA's building property system. These data include each building number with address; type of jurisdiction; and square footage and number of personnel to assist FPS to bill for its services, among other things. FPS personnel then input this information into its systems electronically. MegaCenters—the four regional dispatch centers within FPS that are the primary focal points for incident notification (see figure 1)—use the data to direct calls concerning building incidents and emergencies to FPS personnel as well as state and local law enforcement agencies.

Source: GAO.

As a general practice, MegaCenters make direct radio calls for incident response to FPS personnel and telephone calls to state and local law enforcement agencies. FPS instructs tenants to contact the MegaCenter by calling 1-877-4FPS-411 and, in areas where FPS responders cannot provide an immediate response; tenants are often directed to also dial 911. (See fig. 2.)

Figure 2: Notification and Response Actions Following an Incident at an FPS-Protected Facility

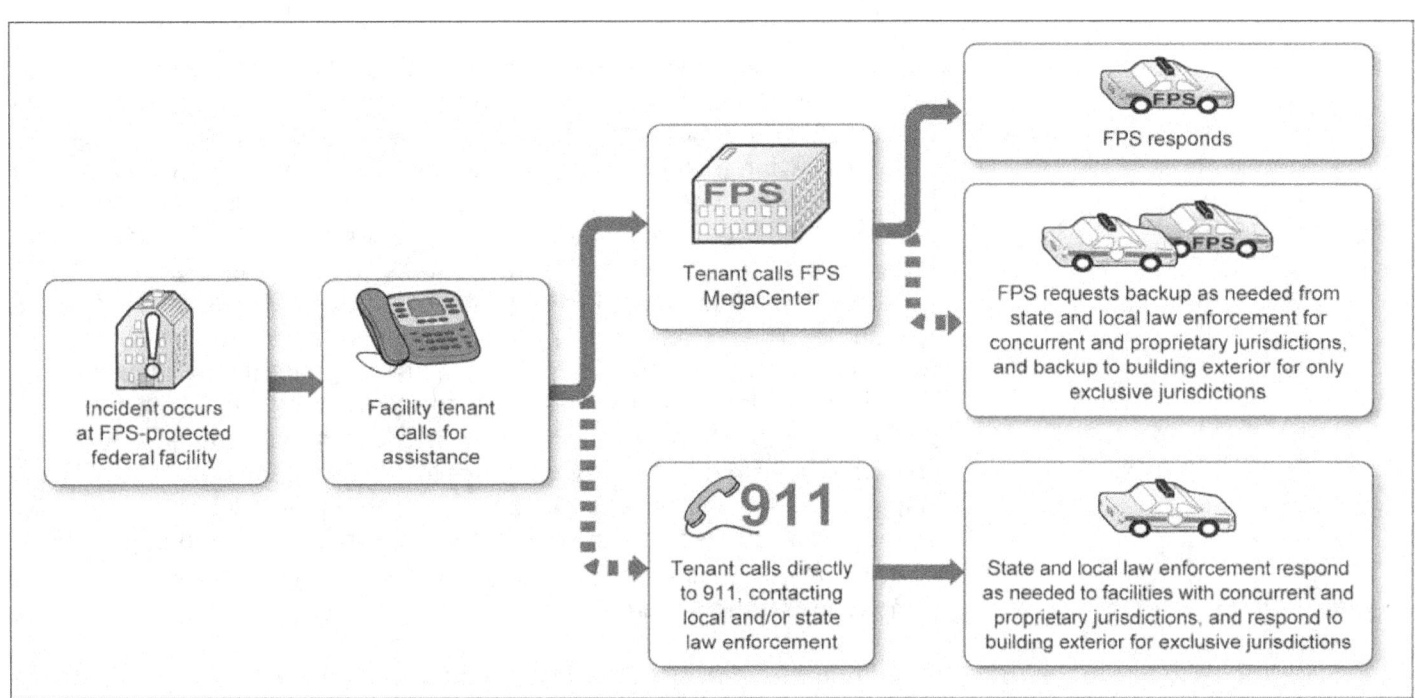

Source: GAO.

In this report, we assess GSA and FPS's processes against GAO's collaboration key practices and internal control standards. Our previous work has broadly defined collaboration as any joint activity that is intended to produce more public value than could be produced when organizations act alone.[10] We have found that key practices for collaboration include:

- identifying and addressing needs by leveraging resources to support the common outcome and, where necessary, identifying opportunities to leverage resources;

- agreeing upon agency roles and responsibilities; and

---

[10]GAO, *Results-Oriented Government: Practices That Can Help Enhance and Sustain Collaboration among Federal Agencies*, GAO-06-15 (Washington, D.C.: Oct. 21, 2005).

- establishing compatible policies, procedures, and other means to operate across agency boundaries.

Additionally, agencies can strengthen their commitment to work collaboratively by articulating their agreements in formal documents, such as an MOU. We have also reported that organizations may face a range of barriers when they attempt to collaborate with other organizations. One such barrier stems from agencies' concerns about protecting jurisdiction over missions. In addition, interagency collaboration is often hindered by incompatible procedures, processes, data, and computer systems. GAO has identified standards in facility protection that provide a framework for guiding agencies' efforts in this area, such as establishing a means of coordinating and sharing information with other government entities and the private sector.[11] Finally, standards for controls over information processing come from GAO's *Standards for Internal Control in the Federal Government*. According to these standards, internal control is a major part of managing an organization and comprises the plans, methods, and procedures used to meet missions, goals, and objectives.[12] Internal control standards specific for information systems help ensure the completeness and accuracy of data.

Some other federal agencies provide their own law enforcement at their facilities. These include the Department of Veterans Affairs (VA) Police, National Park Service (NPS) law enforcement within the Department of the Interior, and Smithsonian Institution (SI) Police. VA Police provide law enforcement duties to the 152 VA Medical Centers (VAMC).[13] U.S. Park Police is a unit of the National Park Service, with jurisdiction in all National Park Service areas and certain other federal and state lands.[14] U.S. Park Police provides law enforcement services to designated areas within the National Park Service (primarily in the District of Columbia, New York City, and San Francisco, California metropolitan areas). Additionally, Law Enforcement Park Rangers, belonging to the "Visitor

---

[11]GAO, *Homeland Security: Further Actions Needed to Coordinate Federal Agencies' Facility Protection Efforts and Promote Key Practices*, GAO-05-49 (Washington, D.C.: Nov. 30, 2004).

[12]GAO, *Standards for Internal Control in the Federal Government*, GAO/AIMD-00-21.3.1. (Washington, D.C.: November 1999).

[13]38 U. S. C. § 902.

[14]16 U. S. C. § 1A-6(b).

and Resource Protection Division" within the National Park Service, are authorized to carry firearms, conduct investigations, make arrests, and serve warrants pursuant to law and policy. Protection and security services at Smithsonian Institution facilities are provided by the Smithsonian Police.[15]

FPS Uses Various Approaches to Collaborate with State and Local Law Enforcement, but Jurisdictional Data on Federal Facilities Are Incomplete

FPS's Approach Involves a Variety of MOUs, Reliance on Long-standing Relationships, Guidance, and Other Initiatives

FPS uses a variety of methods to collaborate with state and local law enforcement, ranging from establishing MOUs to document agreement on roles and responsibilities with some, to relying on long-standing working relationships with others. FPS also has guidance and various other efforts under way related to coordination with state and local law enforcement. More specifically, FPS reported that it had 21 signed MOUs with state and local law enforcement agencies across the United States as of September 2011.[16] For example, there is an MOU for radio frequency usage in Alabama; MOUs for arrest authority on properties adjacent to federal property in California and Florida; and MOUs for mutual aid in the District of Columbia and Georgia, such as FPS's reciprocal support agreement with Metropolitan Atlanta Rapid Transit Authority. MOUs are mechanisms that can be used to formalize key practices in agency collaboration such as agreeing on roles and responsibilities, including

---

[15]40 U. S. C. § 6306.

[16]We did not determine the total universe of state and local law enforcement jurisdictions where FPS-protected properties are located.

leadership, and to establish compatible policies, procedures, and other means to operate across agency boundaries.[17]

While FPS has often found MOUs helpful, the general consensus among FPS officials was that effective coordination did not depend on having MOUs. FPS prefers a flexible approach of pursuing MOUs only when it determines they are needed, as opposed to seeking them in all cases. FPS's Director stated that FPS has generally not found it necessary to create written documents, requirements, or MOUs because FPS has always received good cooperation from state and local law enforcement agencies when their assistance was needed. For example, in some jurisdictions such as the suburbs surrounding the District of Columbia, FPS has no MOUs with state and local law enforcement agencies but has regular contact and longstanding mutual aid relationships. In addition, several FPS Regional Directors highlighted the importance of local response to incidents in and around federal facilities in rural areas because of the lack of FPS staff at these locations and noted that their informal relationships have worked successfully because state and local law enforcement agencies were consistently reliable in their response to these locations. FPS officials stated that mandating the pursuance of MOUs with all law enforcement entities would not be in the best interest of effectiveness and efficiency and would increase the burden on already task-saturated FPS staff. In addition, it is generally up to state and local law enforcement agencies as to whether they would be willing to enter into an MOU with a federal agency.

With regard to long-standing working relationships and regular contact with state and local law enforcement, FPS Inspectors and Regional Directors have developed relationships with state and local law enforcement agencies and collaborate on different levels. Regional Directors in all 11 FPS regions stated that their offices routinely had direct contact with state and local law enforcement agencies at multiple types of security meetings such as the Federal Executive Boards, joint terrorism

---

[17]GAO-06-15.

task forces, and regional fusion center meetings.[18] Attendance by both state and local law enforcement agencies and FPS at these meetings establishes mutually reinforcing or joint strategies designed to help align activities, core processes, and resources to achieve a common outcome. For example, FPS participates in monthly meetings of the Law Enforcement Working Group of the Atlanta Downtown Improvement District. State and local law enforcement chiefs or deputy chiefs from the surrounding area, officials from 15 local colleges, and officials from other federal agencies participate. According to an FPS regional official, the group acts as a "force multiplier" to fight crime within the district, which includes GSA-controlled facilities. FPS officials also have discussions with state and local law enforcement agencies as needed during operational planning associated with special events such as the Olympics, protests, and parades.

FPS also has guidance for FPS staff and other efforts under way to collaborate with state and local law enforcement. Regional Directors are responsible for carrying out FPS policy and guidance, and state that many of these written policies contain directives for collaboration with state and local law enforcement. One such directive is FPS Directive 15.1.2.1, Law Enforcement Authority and Powers, which outlines the scope of law enforcement authority on federal property. Other policies that reference state and local law enforcement agencies' coordination include FPS's Regional Information Sharing Program, Detention and Arrest, and Joint Terrorism Task Force Policy, among others. Best practices and lessons learned are also communicated throughout FPS regions with weekly regional director conference calls, a regional director's council that meets monthly, and yearly Regional Director conferences.

---

[18]The Federal Executive Boards, established by Presidential Directive in 1961, are a forum for communication and collaboration among federal agencies outside of Washington, D.C. Joint terrorism task forces (JTTFs) are small cells of highly trained, locally based investigators, analysts, linguists, special weapons and tactics experts, and other specialists from dozens of U.S. law enforcement and intelligence agencies. JTTFs are used as a multi-agency effort by the U.S. Department of Justice and the Federal Bureau of Investigation to combine the resources of federal, state, and local law enforcement. Fusion centers serve as focal points within the state and local environment for the receipt, analysis, gathering, and sharing of threat-related information between the federal government and state, local, tribal, territorial, and private sector partners.

In addition to guidance, FPS added three new positions in fiscal year 2011 intended to improve communication and standardization across FPS by coordinating with federal, state, and local law enforcement officials to reduce crime at, and potential threats to, federal facilities. These positions are titled Assistant Director for Field Operations (ADFO) for west, central, and east operations. The ADFO will be a spokesman for FPS, representing the Director in his or her designated area.

Other initiatives employed by FPS include collaborative operations to avert or obstruct potential threats inside the facility, such as the presence of unauthorized persons, or potentially disruptive or dangerous activities, such as potential terrorist operations and criminal activity in and around federal buildings. Using a combination of law enforcement agencies is consistent with facility protection key practices to establish a means of coordinating and sharing information with other government entities. These operations begin with planning meetings involving FPS and any other federal, state, and local law enforcement agencies that may be called upon to assist. The operations combine physical security expertise and law enforcement authority into an enhanced security team to provide a visual deterrent at FPS-protected facilities. The combined team then selects a federal building for which FPS has security oversight and provides a highly visible presence for a select period of time with patrol operations, explosive detection dog sweeps, and an enhanced security posture. As a means to leverage resources, FPS has collaborated with state and local law enforcement to assist in conducting these operations by enlisting their support in Chicago, Illinois; New York, New York; Newark, New Jersey; and the District of Columbia.

Like FPS, Other Federal Agencies Use a Variety of Methods to Collaborate with State and Local Law Enforcement

Other federal organizations with law enforcement responsibilities similar to FPS also used a variety of methods to collaborate with state and local law enforcement. For example, VA has a policy requiring all locations of VA-controlled property to have formally documented MOUs with state and local law enforcement agencies to ensure timely backup support for VA Police officers.[19] VA headquarters officials stated that MOUs are useful because VA Police typically transport detainees to state and local law enforcement agencies for arrest and processing, while state and local law

---

[19]Department of Veterans Affairs: *Security and Law Enforcement VA Handbook 0730* (Washington, D.C.: Aug. 11, 2000).

enforcement agencies typically provide first response to leased property under VA control. However, VA Police reported they cannot provide mutual aid to state and local law enforcement agencies on non-VA controlled property because existing law[20] limits the authority of Department police officers to VA property.

According to U.S. Park Police headquarters officials, the Park Police has MOUs with federal, state, and local law enforcement including a longstanding formal relationship with the District of Columbia Metropolitan Police Department (MPD). Some of the MOUs are for events and are short-term, such as the last presidential inauguration in the District of Columbia. The U.S. Park Police also stated they have MOUs that are formal incident response plans, which outline the roles and responsibilities of the various entities. In the District of Columbia, the U.S. Park Police responded to the U.S. Holocaust Museum shooting incident in 2009 and have provided service to the Kennedy Center for the Performing Arts for a fee.

According to a Smithsonian Institution headquarters official, the Smithsonian police rely on MPD and the Park Police to arrest and process suspects in the District of Columbia. Aside from a limited MOU with the District of Columbia, MPD[21] the Smithsonian police does not have MOUs with other law enforcement agencies. In the District of Columbia region as well as nationally, Smithsonian police rely on informal relationships with state and local law enforcement agencies for coordination of law enforcement at Smithsonian-controlled property. However, Smithsonian police officials stated they cannot provide mutual aid— due to lack of authority—to state and local law enforcement agencies on non-Smithsonian-controlled property.

---

[20]38 U. S. C. § 902.

[21]The MOU assists the Metropolitan Police Department. D.C. to conduct crime prevention and law enforcement activities for specific instances or periods of time specified by the Smithsonian Institution's Office of Protective Services. The MOU allows officers from the National Zoo in Washington, D.C. to direct traffic in the immediate surroundings of the Zoo or in the instances of hot pursuit for example, to take action from outside the perimeter of the Zoo if appropriate to protect the Zoo's property, visitors, and animals.

State and Local Law Enforcement Generally Willing to Assist with Protecting Federal Facilities

Our questionnaire of state and local law enforcement agencies and follow-up discussions showed a general willingness of those that replied to respond to incidents at federal facilities. For example, 48 of 52 agencies that answered the question replied that they would respond to calls that dispatch to a federally occupied (owned and/or leased) building, and 27 of 44 had actually responded to a federally occupied building since 2007. As for MOUs, 11 of 43 agencies that answered the question reported having formal MOUs with FPS and 4 of 40 reported having informal agreements. (See table 1.) Four state and local law enforcement agencies stated that they would decline to respond to an incident at a federal building in their jurisdiction. Three of these four law enforcement agencies were sheriff or highway patrol entities that stated that they are not the first responders to incidents at the facilities in question and that there were local police available for response. A fourth questionnaire responder did not clarify why it answered negatively; however, additional inquiry with the federal property owner in this law enforcement's jurisdiction stated the particular law enforcement agency did coordinate and respond to calls at the property. Only one state and local law enforcement agency replied that it was denied access to a federal building when responding to an incident within its jurisdiction; however, it declined to clarify the specific instance in which it was denied access. The only law enforcement agency that answered it had declined to respond to a call dispatched at a federally occupied (owned and/or leased) building, later clarified that the answer applied to non-GSA-controlled facilities such as buildings of Department of Defense and other federal agencies. Table 1 shows the specific questions and responses provided by state and local law enforcement.

Table 1: State and Local Law Enforcement Agencies' Responses to Selected Questions in GAO's Structured Questionnaire Regarding FPS Collaboration

Questions[a]	Answers		
	Yes	No	No answer
To your knowledge, are there federal buildings located within your jurisdiction?[b]	55	1	1
Would your law enforcement entity respond to calls that dispatches to a federally occupied (owned and/or leased) building?	48	4	5
Since 2007, has your law enforcement entity been denied access into federally occupied (owned and/or leased) building in response to an incident under your entity's purview (proprietary of the state or local government, or concurrent with the federal government)?	1	38	18
Since 2007, has your law enforcement entity responded to a call that dispatches to a federally occupied (owned and/or leased) building?	27	17	13

Questions[a]	Answers		
	Yes	No	No answer
Since 2007, has your law enforcement entity declined to respond to a call that dispatches to a federally occupied (owned and/or leased) building?	1	43	13
Since 2007, does your law enforcement entity have any formal memorandums of understanding (MOUs) with the U.S. Department of Homeland Security, Federal Protective Service?	11	32	14
Does your law enforcement entity have any informal agreements with the U.S. Department of Homeland Security, Federal Protective Service?	4	36	17

Source: GAO structured questionnaire of state and local law enforcement agencies.

[a]Not every respondent answered every question.

[b]Although we selected our respondents based on addresses of federal buildings located in their probable geographic jurisdictions, upon further examination, one respondent noted that a building address we chose was actually one street out of its jurisdiction. Therefore it answered that it had no federal buildings in its area of jurisdiction.

FPS's Approach Is Reasonable and Consistent with Key Practices

Overall, the variety of efforts FPS has under way reflects a reasonable approach to collaboration, especially when combined with results we found from our questionnaire of state and local law enforcement agencies. The practice of maintaining working relationships and having regular contact with state and local law enforcement officials establishes mutually reinforcing or joint strategies designed to help align activities, core processes, and resources to achieve a common outcome. The MOUs that FPS has in place are mechanisms consistent with facilitating key practices in agency collaboration, such as defining and agreeing to roles and responsibilities. Establishing compatible policies, procedures, and other means to operate across agency boundaries are key practices that can help enhance and sustain collaboration. Pursuing MOUs on an as-needed basis is also consistent with how other federal law enforcement agencies approach collaboration. Performing operations such as extra patrol activities using a combination of law enforcement agencies is consistent with facility protection key practices to establish a means of coordinating and sharing information with other government entities.

Missing Jurisdictional Data Are of Concern, and Data Inconsistencies with GSA Are Being Addressed

Although FPS's approach to collaboration is reasonable, issues related to data quality arose during our review. Specifically, we found that FPS lacked complete data from GSA on the type of jurisdiction (e.g., concurrent or exclusive) for about one-third of the buildings FPS protects, making it difficult to ensure that it is addressing the full scope of issues related to jurisdictional roles and responsibilities. At the end of our review,

GSA officials informed us that they had made significant progress addressing this issue. More specifically, when we reviewed the property list that GSA provided to FPS in December 2011—which is provided on a weekly basis—about thirty-four percent of the properties lacked recorded jurisdictions, including blank and pending jurisdiction categories. (See table 2.)

Table 2: Jurisdiction of Properties under the Control of GSA with FPS Responsibility

Jurisdiction[a,b]	Number of GSA Properties	Percentage
Pending	1594	18
Exclusive	329	4
Concurrent	662	7
Partial	31	0
Proprietary	4969	55
Combined	21	0
Blank[b]	1432	16
Total	**9038**	**100**

Source: GAO analysis of GSA data.

[a]GSA provides the following guidance when assigning jurisdiction to its properties: Pending: requires value assignment in the database; Exclusive: the U.S. enjoys exclusive legislative jurisdiction and the state has no legislative jurisdiction except for minor forms of taxation; Concurrent: both the U.S. and a state enjoy complete legislative jurisdiction; Partial: the state has selectively ceded certain aspects of legislative jurisdiction to the U.S; Proprietary: the state exercises complete legislative jurisdiction and the U.S. is considered only a property holder; Combined: any location at which more than one of the above jurisdictions exist.

[b]Blank represents number of facilities missing GSA jurisdictional data.

GSA officials stated that they were aware of the numerous blank data fields pertaining to jurisdictions and that they were trying to individually assess these fields building by building. They further stated that it was a time-consuming process that included reviewing individual property historical records. GSA officials stated they had made progress and the jurisdictions that have not been identified were down to 2 percent. However, these data had not yet been added to GSA's building property system or contained in the electronic files GSA sends to FPS weekly. GSA officials also stated the jurisdictional field on the GSA property list was not in the top fifty fields that the agency typically monitors because of the large number of data fields, although the officials recognized the importance of this field to FPS.

During our review, we found no instances in which state or local law enforcement exceeded their jurisdictional authority. In some instances, state and local law enforcement responded to the perimeter of buildings with exclusive jurisdiction for matters such as traffic accidents and suspicious packages. FPS officials said that state and local law enforcement may also be granted access if officers are in pursuit of a suspect. Furthermore, FPS officials said that inspectors and GSA staff at the building level generally know the jurisdiction of the individual buildings for which they are responsible.

Nonetheless, given that facilities of exclusive jurisdiction are unique because state and local law enforcement agencies generally have no law enforcement authority on these properties, incomplete data leaves FPS less equipped to define and agree to respective roles and responsibilities with regard to state and local law enforcement collaboration. An additional effect of not having these data is that FPS lacks assurance that, in relying on state and local law enforcement to respond to incidents at federal facilities, it is not creating a situation where these entities may be exercising police authority where they lack such authority as in the case of exclusive jurisdiction properties. In addition, having incomplete data is inconsistent with established standards for internal control over data systems, including those standards that relate to accuracy and completeness. While only 4 percent of GSA's inventory was known to be of exclusive jurisdiction, 34 percent of GSA's inventory had incomplete data on the type of jurisdiction in GSA's building property system.

In our review, we also found inconsistencies between FPS and GSA data on buildings and their locations—6 of the 11 FPS regions reported that the GSA list does not match the current property inventory. One FPS regional official stated that GSA does not keep the property list as current as FPS needs; changes occur but are not captured by GSA. For example, the official stated that in his region, agencies sign leases about a dozen times a year without FPS's knowledge or timely notice. FPS officials noted that the overall number could be greater across all FPS regions. The current MOU between GSA and FPS calls for a pre-lease assessment of the building by FPS, but these assessments cannot be completed if FPS is unaware of the new lease.[22] Another FPS regional official stated that the region uses its own building list, which is updated by FPS regularly as information becomes available. A third FPS official stated that the GSA list does not capture changes to buildings with a security risk level of 1 or 2 as quickly as FPS needs.[23] A fourth regional official stated that the region relies on a combination of building lists from GSA, FPS provided lists, and its own regional list. This official stated these lists often do not reconcile because of changes that are not updated in a timely manner. In addition, a majority of state and local law enforcement agencies we sent questions to replied that they did not identify the jurisdiction of the individual federal buildings in their geographic areas, while three entities replied that they only identified some building jurisdictions.

GSA officials recognize that the exchange of building data with FPS is an issue. GSA stated that only recently did it have the ability to cross-reference and address these differences, and is working with FPS to correct them. For example, in 2011, GSA and FPS held working groups to begin to improve the building property list, and established a permanent GSA liaison in FPS's headquarters to improve data coordination. Although this effort is still in progress and data inconsistencies remain, GSA and FPS are addressing concerns about data inconsistencies. Further, GSA and FPS are currently negotiating a new MOU that is expected to be finalized in early 2012. GSA officials told us that the new MOU will include an agreement on sharing information, such as the building data, and specifically sharing information at the regional level. FPS and GSA did not indicate whether the revised MOU would address the aforementioned issue related to incomplete jurisdictional data. However, it would seem that addressing this issue in conjunction with revising the MOU would ensure that data shared were not only consistent, but more complete as well.

[22]The current MOU between FPS and GSA began on June 1, 2006, and was valid for 2 years. However, the MOU states that upon expiration of the initial term, the MOU will automatically be renewed and will remain in full force and effect until modified in writing, executed by both parties, or terminated by either party upon 90 days' written notice to the other party.

[23]Each federal building is assessed a security risk level, with Level 1 as lowest and Level 5 as highest. FPS uses Interagency Security Committee guidelines to determine a facility's security level, which in turn determines the level of physical protection services needed at each of the approximately 9,000 buildings.

Conclusions

FPS's approach to collaborating with state and local law enforcement is reasonable and consistent with key practices in that the approach uses mechanisms such as MOUs to document agreements on roles and responsibilities in some cases, long-standing working relationships, written guidance to FPS staff, joint operations, and other initiatives to promote mutual collaboration. Other federal organizations with law enforcement responsibilities similar to FPS—such as VA, U.S. Park Police, and Smithsonian—also use a variety of methods for collaboration with state and local law enforcement. State and local law enforcement agencies we contacted were generally willing to assist FPS with incidents at federal facilities. Related to the quality of data exchanged between FPS and GSA on buildings and their locations, FPS and GSA had taken action to address data inconsistency issues. However, as of the end of our review, FPS still lacked complete data from GSA on whether the jurisdictions of about one-third of the buildings FPS protects are exclusive, concurrent, or proprietary. Having these data is important because state and local law enforcement generally have no authority to enforce state and local law on properties of exclusive jurisdiction. At the end of our review, GSA informed us that it had made progress with addressing this issue. GSA and FPS are negotiating a revised MOU that will include agreement on sharing information such as the building data. As such, addressing the issue related to incomplete data on jurisdictions, in conjunction with revising the MOU, would ensure that data were not only consistent, but more complete as well. Otherwise, FPS would remain less equipped to define and agree to respective roles and responsibilities as it proceeds with its efforts to rely on state and local law enforcement for assistance in responding to incidents at federal facilities.

Recommendations for Executive Action

In conjunction with the revised MOU that is being developed between GSA and FPS, we recommend the Administrator of GSA ensure that efforts to identify the jurisdictions of all GSA buildings are completed and that these data are provided to FPS so that FPS is better equipped to manage jurisdictional roles and responsibilities at GSA buildings.

Agency Comments and Our Evaluation

We provided a draft of this report to GSA, DHS, DOI, VA, and Smithsonian Institution for their review and comment. GSA provided written comments, which are reprinted in appendix II. GSA concurred with our recommendation that the Administrator of GSA ensure that efforts to identify the jurisdictions of all GSA buildings are completed, and that these data are provided to FPS so that FPS is better equipped to manage jurisdictional roles and responsibilities at GSA buildings. DHS provided a letter, reprinted in appendix III, describing its efforts to collaborate with state and local law enforcement. DHS also provided technical comments, which we incorporated, as appropriate. DOI, VA, and the Smithsonian Institution provided minor technical comments, via email, which we incorporated, as appropriate.

As agreed with your office, unless you publicly announce the contents of this report earlier, we plan no further distribution until 30 days from the report date. At that time, we will send copies to the Secretary of Homeland Security, the Director of FPS, the Administrator of GSA, the Secretary of the Interior, the Secretary of Veterans Affairs, and Secretary of the Smithsonian Institution. In addition, the report will be available at no charge on the GAO's Web site at http://www.gao.gov.

If you, or your staff, have any questions about this report, please contact me at (202) 512-2834 or goldsteinm@gao.gov. Contact points for our Offices of Congressional Relations and Public Affairs may be found on the last page of this report. GAO staff who made key contributions to this report are listed in appendix IV.

Sincerely yours,

Mark Goldstein
Director
Physical Infrastructure Issues

Appendix I: Objective, Scope and Methodology

To assess the Federal Protective Service's (FPS) efforts to collaborate with state and local law enforcement for assistance in responding to incidents at federal facilities, we reviewed FPS data on buildings protected, staffing, procedures, and memorandums of understanding (MOUs). We also reviewed relevant federal facility building data from the General Services Administration (GSA) including for example, each building number with address; type of jurisdiction; and square footage and number of personnel, among other things. We interviewed FPS officials throughout the regions, and FPS and GSA officials at their respective agency's headquarters in Washington, D.C., regarding the processes and procedures for exchanging these data. We reviewed the building data for completeness, but did not verify the accuracy of the information contained for each building. To ensure we were assessing the exact data that FPS uses, we requested data samples for fiscal year 2011 from both GSA and FPS and replicated the jurisdiction category results. We assessed the extent to which there were missing jurisdiction assignments by reviewing pending and blank jurisdiction categories. We then assessed GSA and FPS's processes for managing these data against GAO's *Standards for Internal Control in the Federal Government, Homeland Security: Further Actions Needed to Coordinate Federal Agencies' Facility Protection Efforts and Promote Key Practices, and Results-Oriented Government: Practices That Can Help Enhance and Sustain Collaboration among Federal Agencies.* [1] According to GAO's standards for internal control in the federal government, internal control is a major part of managing an organization and comprises the plans, methods, and procedures used to meet missions, goals, and objectives. Internal control, which is synonymous with management control, helps government program managers achieve desired results through effective stewardship of public resources. Control activities—such as reconciliations performed to verify data completeness; an agency's data entry design features contribute to data accuracy; data validation and editing performed to identify erroneous data; and erroneous data that is captured, reported, investigated, and promptly corrected—contribute to data accuracy and completeness. We

---

[1]GAO, *Standards for Internal Control in the Federal Government*, GAO/AIMD-00-21.3.1. (Washington, D.C.: November 1999); GAO, *Homeland Security: Further Actions Needed to Coordinate Federal Agencies' Facility Protection Efforts and Promote Key Practices*, GAO-05-49 (Washington, D.C.: Nov. 30, 2004); GAO, *Results-Oriented Government: Practices That Can Help Enhance and Sustain Collaboration among Federal Agencies*, GAO-06-15 (Washington, D.C.: Oct. 21, 2005).

determined that the data were sufficiently reliable for the purposes of this report.

For comparison with FPS's coordination efforts, we contacted three federal agencies that provide law enforcement at their facilities—the Department of Veterans Affairs (VA), the National Park Service (NPS) within the Department of the Interior, and the Smithsonian Institution (SI). To gain insight into FPS, VA, SI, and NPS coordination with state and local law enforcement agencies, we emailed a self-administered set of 22 structured questions to the heads of 73 state and local law enforcement agencies. Our non-random selection of locations included varying population sizes located in a mixture of metro, urban, and rural areas as defined by the United States Department of Agriculture using the most recent Rural-Urban Continuum Codes for jurisdictions that we determined had FPS, and/or VA, NPS, and SI buildings throughout the United States. The state and local law enforcement agencies we chose included a mix of police, sheriff, highway patrol agencies in each of the 11 FPS regions. We also followed up our email with phone calls to these state and local law enforcement agencies. Not every respondent answered every question related to coordination with FPS, VA Police, U.S. Park Police, and SI police. Additionally, the responses had varying levels of staff within the state and local law enforcement organization reply for the organization. Furthermore, the structured questions were related to coordination with the Federal Protective Service, Veterans Affairs Police, Smithsonian police, and the U.S. Park Police. Although the results of our questions cannot be generalized to the universe of jurisdictions that have interaction with FPS, the results provide key insights on how state and local law enforcement collaborates with FPS to assist with federal facility protection. These results illustrate how FPS relies on these organizations to respond to incidents and collectively, how this multi-faceted approach enabled us to make conclusions whether FPS's approach is reasonable.[2]

Further, we interviewed officials at two FPS MegaCenters—the four regional dispatch centers within FPS that are the primary focal points for initial incident notification—and toured the Suitland, Md., MegaCenter facility. We attended an FPS operational exercise in the District of Columbia. We also interviewed each of the 11 FPS Regional Directors to

---

[2]Results from nonprobablity samples cannot be used to make inferences about a population because in a nonprobability sample, some elements of the population being studied have no chance or an unknown chance of being selected as part of the sample.

determine how their region coordinates with state and local law enforcement entities for the properties in their jurisdiction. We interviewed GSA officials at GSA headquarters in the District of Columbia. We obtained relevant documents pertaining to VA, NPS, and SI collaboration with state and local law enforcement and interviewed agency officials. Lastly, we reviewed prior GAO work, including reports on key practices in interagency collaboration and facility protection.

We conducted this performance audit from February 2011 to March 2012 in accordance with generally accepted government auditing standards. Those standards require that we plan and perform the audit to obtain sufficient, appropriate evidence to provide a reasonable basis for our findings and conclusions based on our audit objectives. We believe that the evidence obtained provides a reasonable basis for our findings and conclusions based on our audit objectives.

The Administrator

March 9, 2012

The Honorable Gene L. Dodaro
Comptroller General of the United States
U.S. Government Accountability Office
Washington, DC 20548

Dear Mr. Dodaro:

The General Services Administration (GSA) appreciates the opportunity to review and comment on the draft report entitled "Federal Protective Service: Better Data on Facility Jurisdictions Needed to Enhance Collaboration of State and Local Law Enforcement," (GAO-12-434). The Government Accountability Office (GAO) recommends that the GSA Administrator ensure that efforts to identify the jurisdictions of all GSA buildings are completed and that data is provided to the Federal Protective Service (FPS).

GSA agrees with the recommendation and has taken action to implement the recommendation. GSA recently processed a database change that will enhance the ability to share information with FPS, including jurisdictional information. Following the recent change, PBS reviewed all active assignments with jurisdiction fields and found that jurisdiction information was available for over 93 percent of active buildings. GSA will continue to provide updated information to FPS.

If you have any additional questions or concerns, please do not hesitate to contact me or Mr. Robert A. Peck, Commissioner, Public Buildings Service, at (202) 501-1100. Staff inquiries may be directed to Ms. Martha Benson, Assistant Commissioner for Real Property Asset Management. Ms. Benson can be reached at (202) 208-7176.

Sincerely,

Martha Johnson
Administrator

Enclosure

cc: Mark Goldstein, Director, Physical Infrastructure Issues

U.S. General Services Administration
1275 First Street, NE
Washington, DC 20417
Telephone: (202) 501-0800
Fax: (202) 219-1243

Appendix III: Comments from Department of Homeland Security

U.S. Department of Homeland Security
Washington, DC 20528

March 13, 2012

Mr. Mark Goldstein
Director, Physical Infrastructure Issues
U.S. Government Accountability Office
441 G Street, NW
Washington, DC 20548

Subject: Draft Report GAO-12-434, "FEDERAL PROTECTIVE SERVICE: Better Data on Facility Jurisdictions Needed to Enhance Collaboration with State and Local Law Enforcement"

Dear Mr. Goldstein:

Thank you for the opportunity to review and comment on this draft report. The U.S. Department of Homeland Security (DHS) appreciates the U.S. Government Accountability Office's (GAO's) work in planning and conducting its review and issuing this report.

The Department is pleased to note GAO's positive acknowledgement of the Federal Protective Service's (FPS's)—located within the National Protection and Program Directorate of DHS—effective approach to collaborating with state and local law enforcement, using Memoranda of Understanding (MOUs), more informal relationships, and other initiatives.

FPS is responsible for the safety of more than a million people who visit over 9,000 General Services Administration (GSA)-controlled facilities each day. Some facilities have proprietary or concurrent jurisdiction—in which authority is shared by state and local police, while others have exclusive jurisdiction—in which only federal law enforcement has authority. Established agreements and partnerships between FPS and other federal, state, and local law enforcement agencies support coordination necessary for protection of these facilities. For example, FPS law enforcement officers generally cover more than 1,000 demonstrations and disturbances and make more than 1,600 arrests annually, many of which require close coordination with other law enforcement organizations.

FPS conducts operations at federal facilities to serve as visual deterrents to potential terrorist operations and criminal activity in and around federal buildings. To ensure information sharing and operational cooperation, FPS engages state and local law enforcement agencies in advance planning and after-action reporting. These operations include law enforcement and security personnel testing and validating the effectiveness of FPS countermeasures, conducting perimeter patrols and explosive detection sweeps, interviewing suspicious persons, and evaluating access control and screening operations. In 2011, FPS conducted

1,933 operations that included more than 10,000 explosives detection sweeps, 7,500 field interviews, and 6,300 screening and access control-post tests.

Since the time of GAO's review, FPS has expanded initiatives cited in the report, further enhancing data sharing with GSA and coordination with state and local law enforcement. For example, FPS issued a revised Law Enforcement Authority and Powers directive in November 2011, which sets forth the law enforcement authority and powers of FPS law enforcement personnel. For each type of jurisdiction, the directive defines specifically what law enforcement actions FPS officers may and may not take at a facility.

In addition, FPS and GSA have an established MOU that defines the services each agency provides to tenants of their facilities, as well as information shared between them. A revision of the MOU is under way, with FPS and GSA working collaboratively to ensure it includes key elements of the partnership, such as information and data sharing. Additionally, a full-time GSA position was established at FPS headquarters and staffed in 2011, with the intent to raise and resolve coordination issues on facility security and improve the quality and transfer of information between GSA and FPS.

In tandem with the revised MOU and the establishment of a full-time GSA position at FPS headquarters, three new field positions were also added and staffed in 2011 to improve communication and coordination between FPS and federal, state, and local law enforcement officials. These new senior executive positions are Assistant Directors for Field Operations, who oversee regional operations. They are responsible for establishing and maintaining close and cooperative working relationships with Agency and Department management officials, government agencies, and other institutions with related interests to advance the mission objectives of the Department.

Although the report does not contain any recommendations specifically directed at DHS, the Department remains committed to continuing its work with interagency partners, such as GSA, to identify and mitigate security-related vulnerabilities at federal facilities, as appropriate. This includes FPS working with GSA to complete efforts to identify the jurisdictions of all GSA buildings and better manage jurisdictional roles and responsibilities.

Again, thank you for the opportunity to review and comment on this draft report. Technical comments were previously provided under separate cover. We look forward to working with you on future Homeland Security issues.

Sincerely,

Jim H. Crumpacker
Director
Departmental GAO-OIG Liaison Office

2

Appendix IV: GAO Contact and Staff Acknowledgments

GAO Contact	Mark Goldstein, (202) 512-2834 or goldsteinm@gao.gov
Staff Acknowledgments	In addition to the contact named above, David Sausville (Assistant Director), Maren McAvoy, and George Depaoli made key contributions to this report. Additionally, Colin Fallon, Kathleen Gilhooly, Hannah Laufe, and Andrew Stavisky aided in this assignment.

www.ingramcontent.com/pod-product-compliance
Lightning Source LLC
Chambersburg PA
CBHW080937290526
45795CB00007BA/2786